AF496576

Those MAGNIFICENT Voyagers *of the Pacific*

Andrew Crowe

Illustrations by Rick Fisher

BATEMAN BOOKS

POLYNESIAN ORIGINS, 3000 BC

Some 5000 years ago, the ancestors of Polynesians were living along the shores of the South China Sea. Here, many of the islands are so close to one another that a sailor can often see the next island long before losing sight of land behind. This sea provided a safe place to learn seagoing skills. Indeed, the people soon became very skilled at sailing boats.

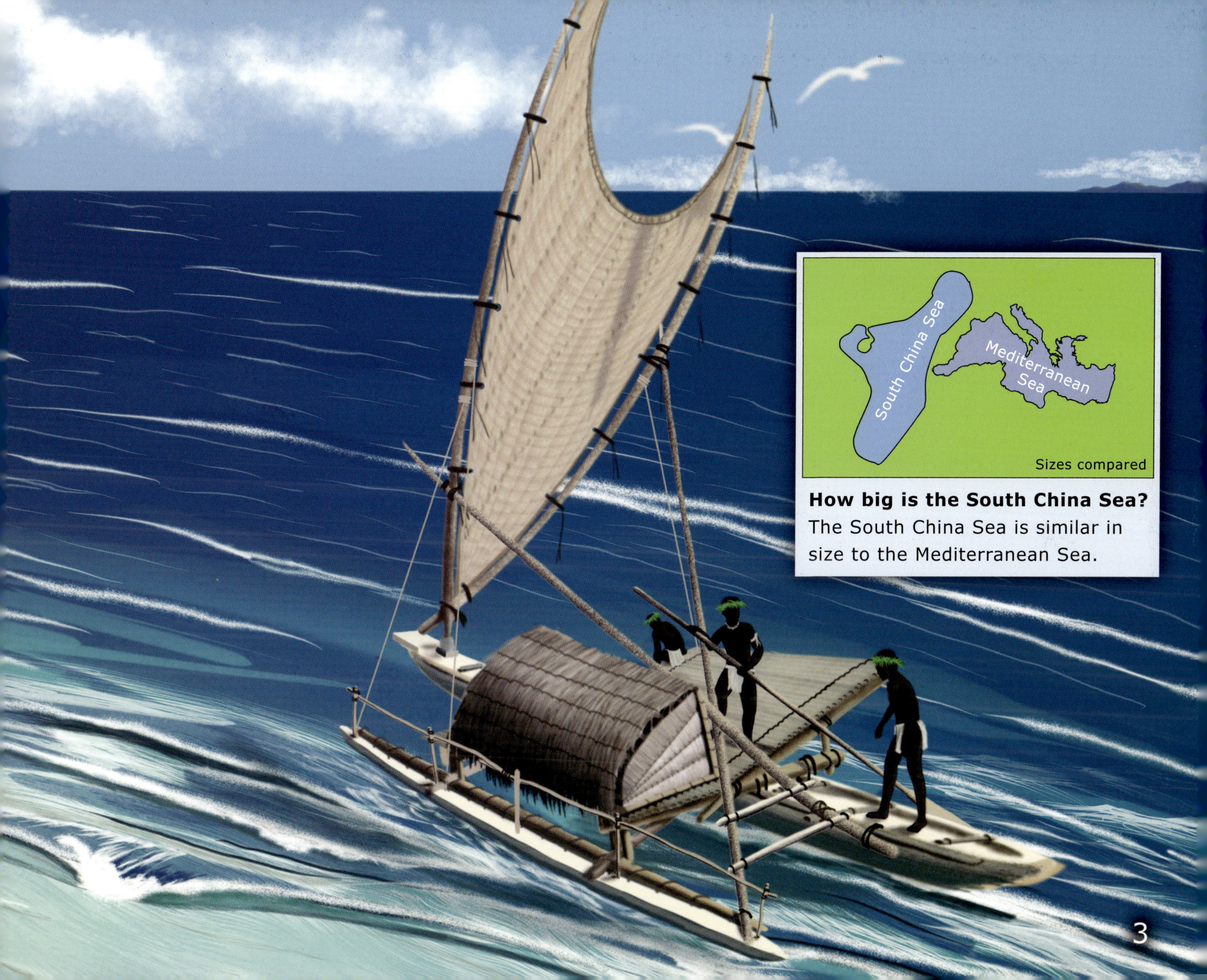

How big is the South China Sea?
The South China Sea is similar in size to the Mediterranean Sea.

MEANWHILE, OVER ON THE OTHER SIDE OF THE WORLD

Meanwhile, over on the other side of the world, others were discovering how to write, and build wheeled vehicles. The people of Egypt were building pyramids and learning how to use a sail to let the wind carry their boats up the River Nile.

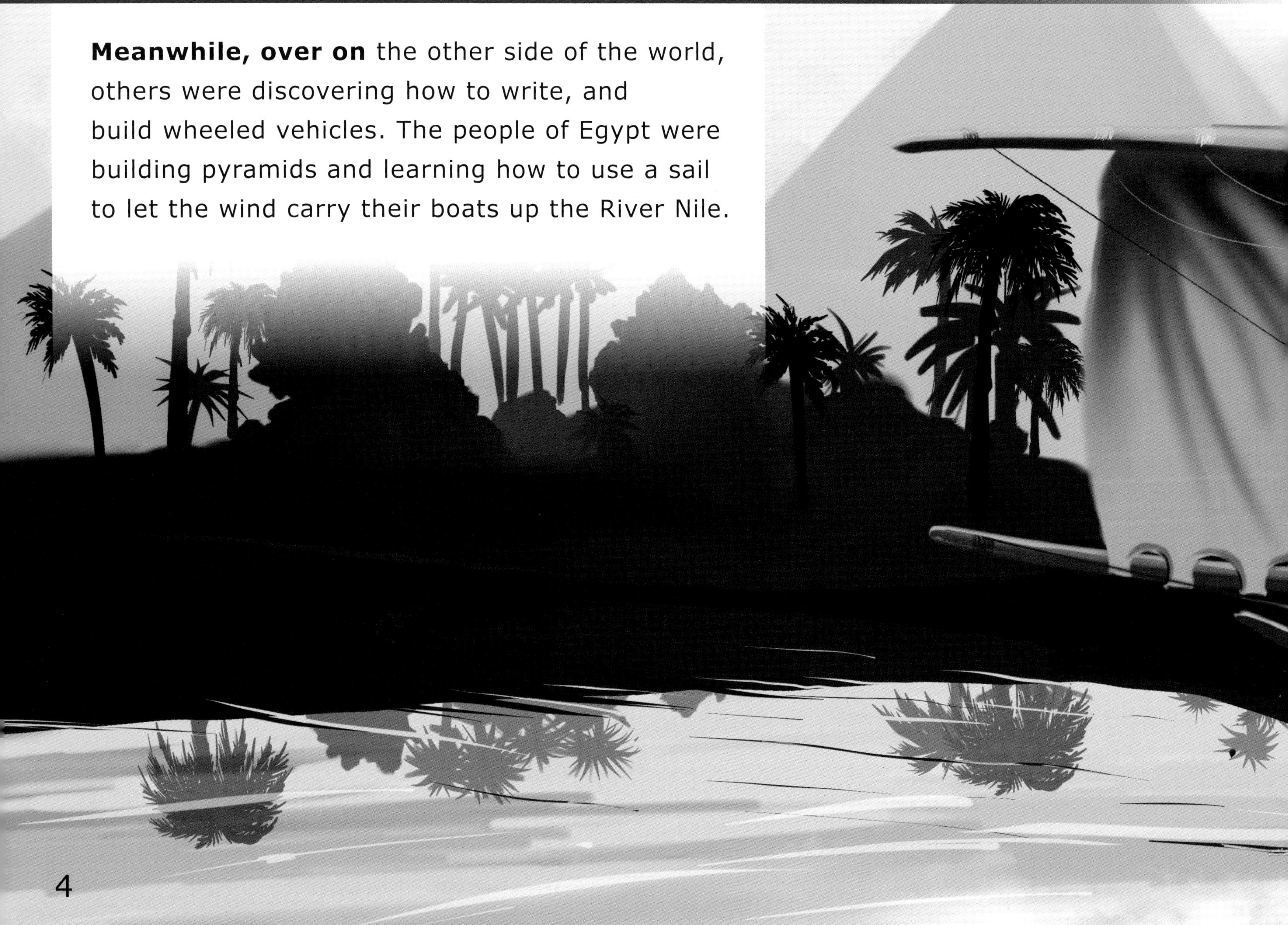

These sailors would go on to use the coast of the Mediterranean Sea as a highway. However, they would always keep close to shore, where they could see land. That way, they would never get lost.

PACIFIC OCEAN, 1500 BC

Some 1500 years passed. By this time, the ancestors of Polynesians had begun to sail much further. They reached as far as the Bismarck Islands, just north of Australia.

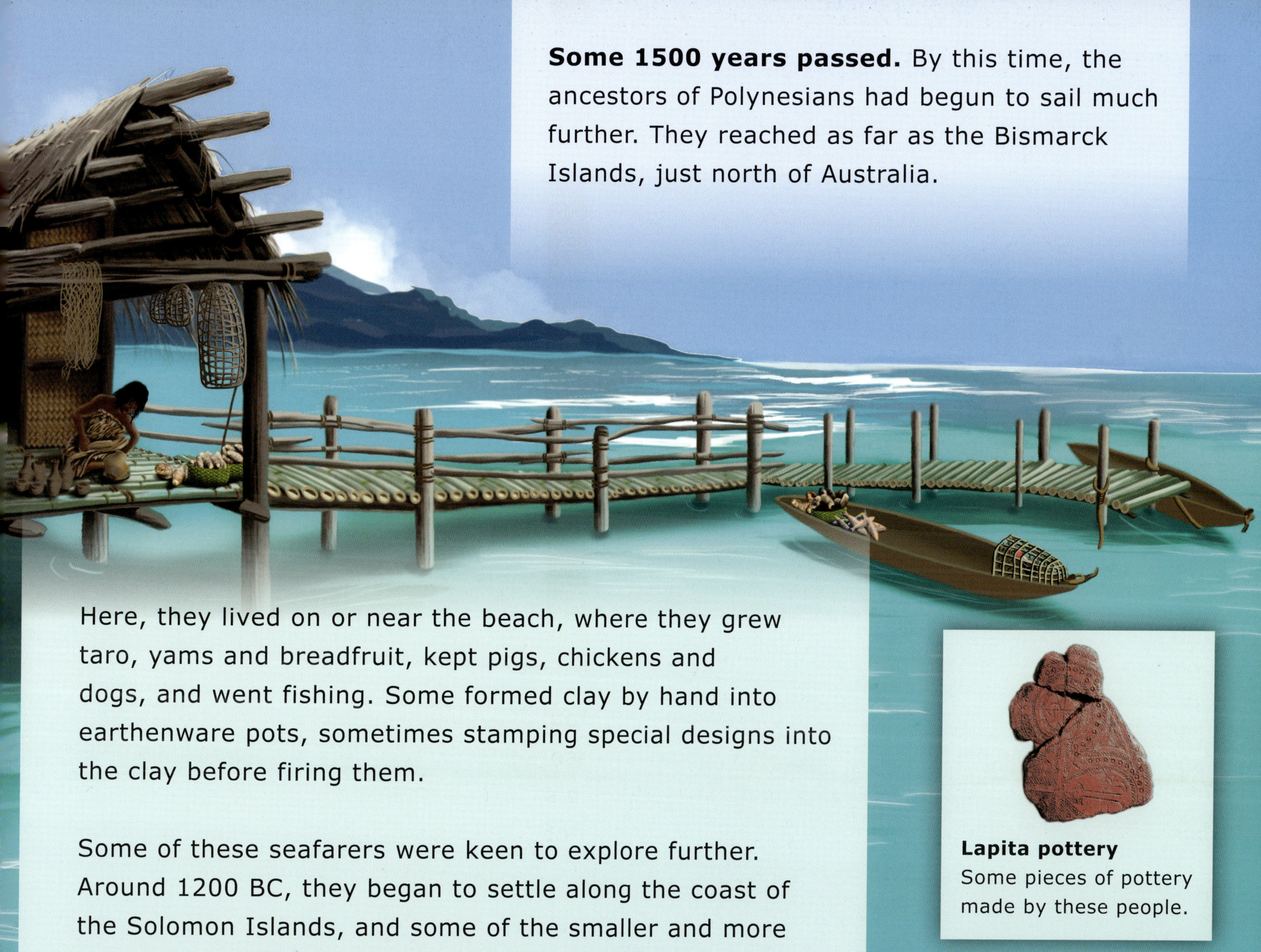

Here, they lived on or near the beach, where they grew taro, yams and breadfruit, kept pigs, chickens and dogs, and went fishing. Some formed clay by hand into earthenware pots, sometimes stamping special designs into the clay before firing them.

Some of these seafarers were keen to explore further. Around 1200 BC, they began to settle along the coast of the Solomon Islands, and some of the smaller and more scattered islands of Vanuatu and New Caledonia.

Lapita pottery
Some pieces of pottery made by these people.

MEANWHILE, OVER ON THE OTHER SIDE OF THE WORLD

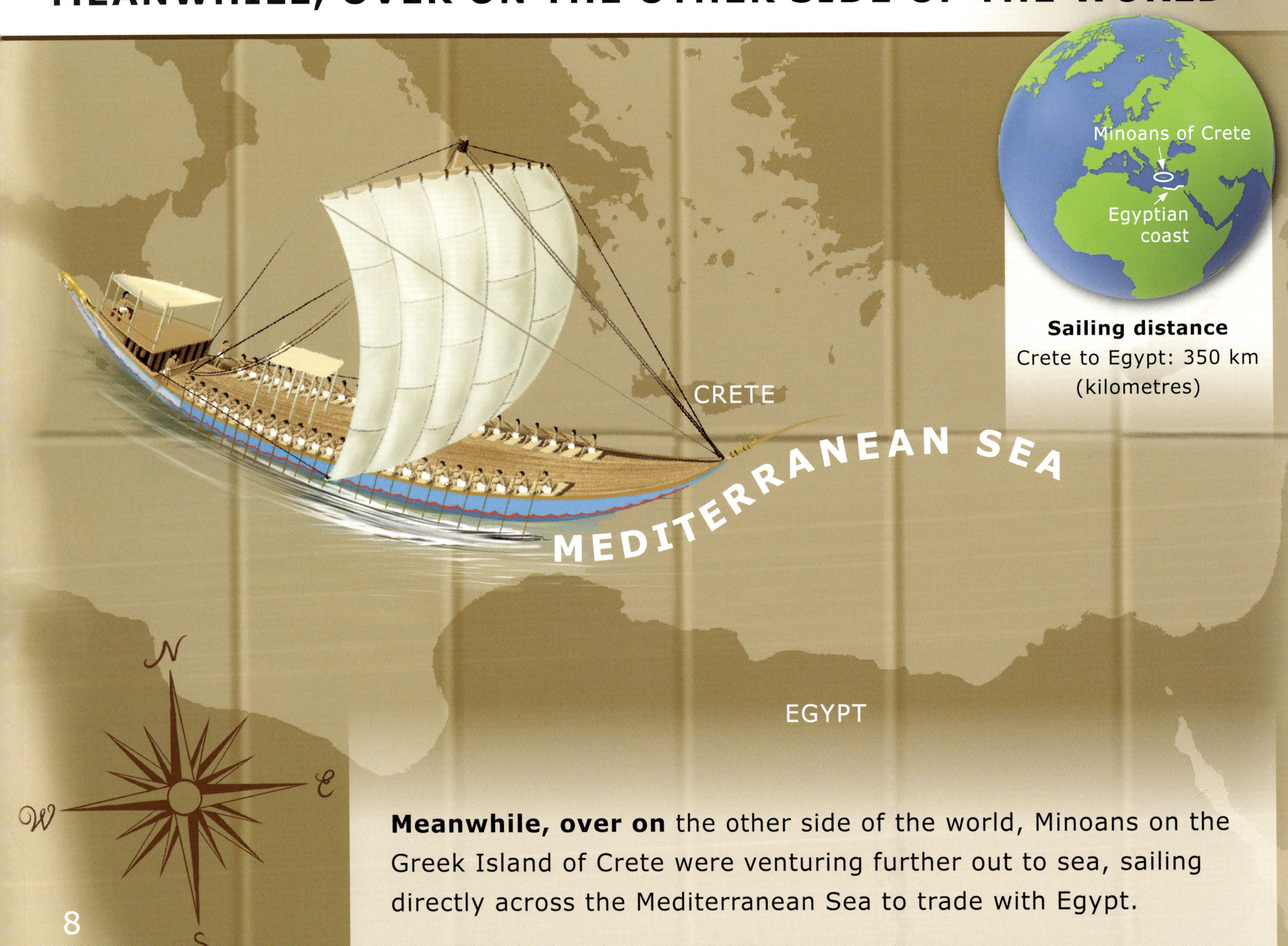

Sailing distance
Crete to Egypt: 350 km
(kilometres)

Meanwhile, over on the other side of the world, Minoans on the Greek Island of Crete were venturing further out to sea, sailing directly across the Mediterranean Sea to trade with Egypt.

And the English had begun to cross the English Channel.

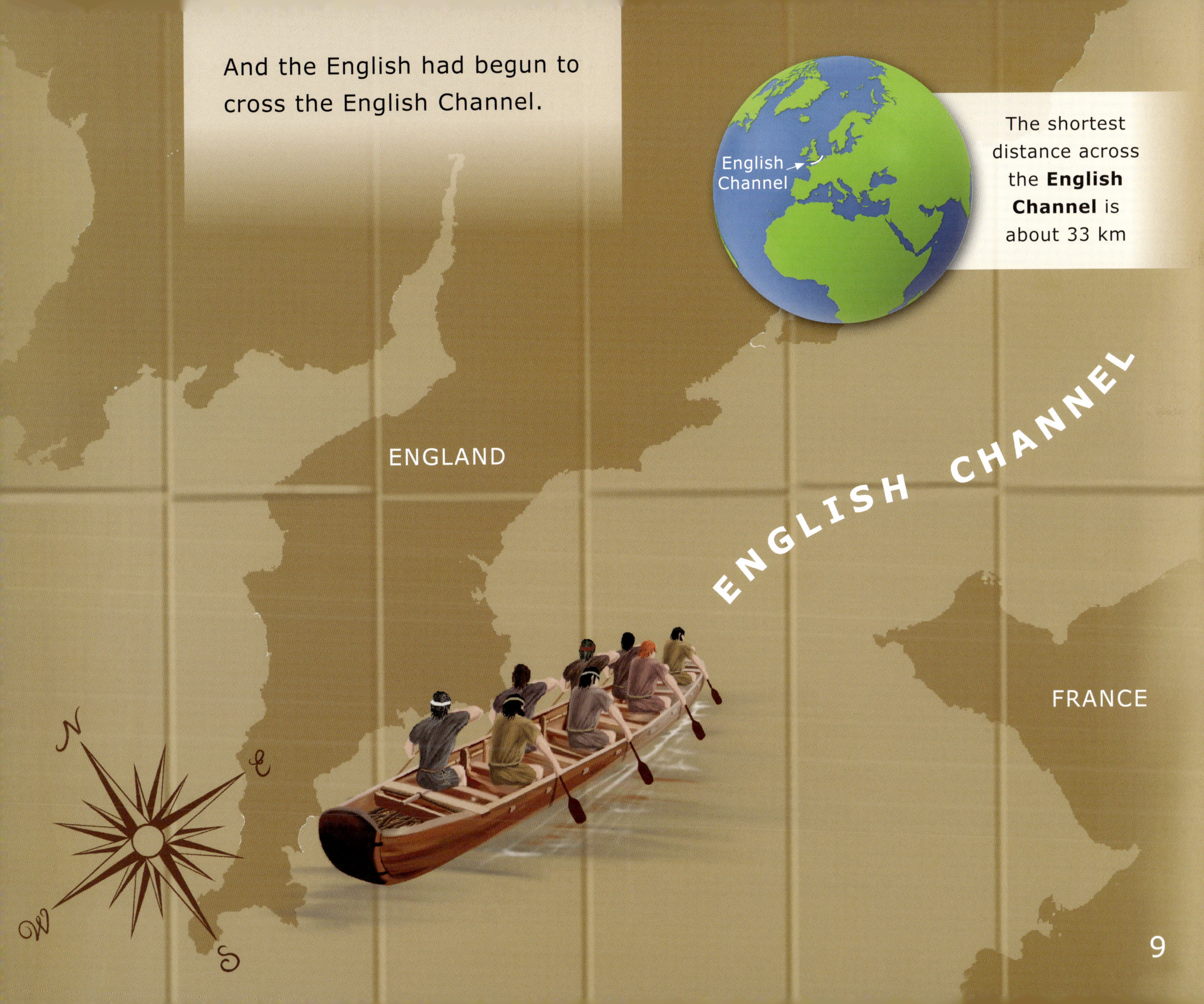

PACIFIC OCEAN, 1000 BC

Another 500 years passed. Now, the ancestors of Polynesians were ready to take a much, much bigger step. They headed some 800 kilometres east to discover islands in Fiji, Tonga and Sāmoa.

With no instruments of navigation, nature was their guide. When flocks of pigeons headed out to sea at around the same time each year in search of wild fruit on other islands, the voyagers knew that more land lay in that direction.

To explore these long distances safely, they would wait for a favourable wind. Whenever a new island was discovered, the explorers had only to wait for the wind to return to its usual direction to carry them back home to share news of their discoveries.

Food and water for the voyage

The voyagers would catch fish along the way, and take with them bananas, breadfruit and taro, some of it fresh, the rest dried or fermented. They would carry coconuts, too, for the food and water they contain.

MEANWHILE, OVER ON THE OTHER SIDE OF THE WORLD

Meanwhile, over on the other side of the world, Phoenician people living at the eastern end of the Mediterranean Sea had become master shipbuilders. They would sail far along the coast and knew the Mediterranean so well that they could take many shortcuts across it.

Why the eyes?
Even today, many Mediterranean fishermen believe that having a pair of eyes on the bow of their boat will help to protect them from harm when they are at sea.

The Mediterranean is an enclosed sea, so the Phoenicians were never out of sight of land for long. This meant that they could not really get lost.

PACIFIC OCEAN AT THE TIME OF CHRIST

After a thousand years of living in the region of Fiji, Tonga and Sāmoa, the islanders were well settled. At first, though, they had found very few wild food plants or land animals, so they had to return to fetch their own crops, chickens, pigs and hunting dogs.

They did find plenty of birds here, though. These birds had never seen a human or dog before, so had no fear of them, making the birds very easy to hunt with nets, spears and hooks. The villagers also caught many kinds of fish and other seafood.

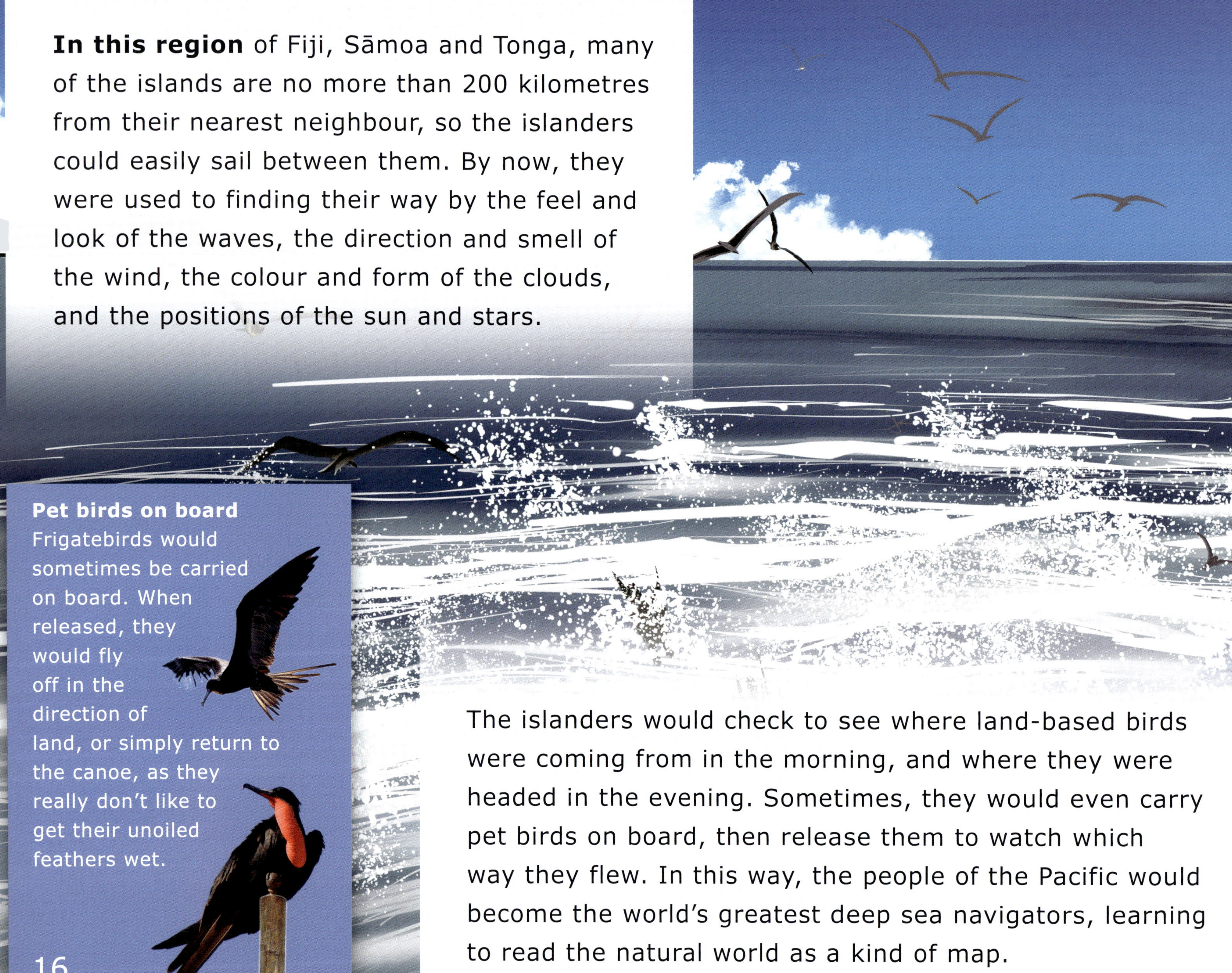

In this region of Fiji, Sāmoa and Tonga, many of the islands are no more than 200 kilometres from their nearest neighbour, so the islanders could easily sail between them. By now, they were used to finding their way by the feel and look of the waves, the direction and smell of the wind, the colour and form of the clouds, and the positions of the sun and stars.

Pet birds on board
Frigatebirds would sometimes be carried on board. When released, they would fly off in the direction of land, or simply return to the canoe, as they really don't like to get their unoiled feathers wet.

The islanders would check to see where land-based birds were coming from in the morning, and where they were headed in the evening. Sometimes, they would even carry pet birds on board, then release them to watch which way they flew. In this way, the people of the Pacific would become the world's greatest deep sea navigators, learning to read the natural world as a kind of map.

MEANWHILE, OVER ON THE OTHER SIDE OF THE WORLD

Meanwhile, over on the other side of the world, others were growing confident enough to cross the Mediterranean Sea more regularly. The Greeks had also learnt how to take shortcuts across the Arabian Sea to reach India without having to hug the coastline. Here, again, there was not much risk of getting lost, for India is a huge target and almost impossible to miss.

Likewise, Egyptian, Indian, Malay and Chinese sailors had now begun making very long voyages along the coast.

Greek voyaging
India

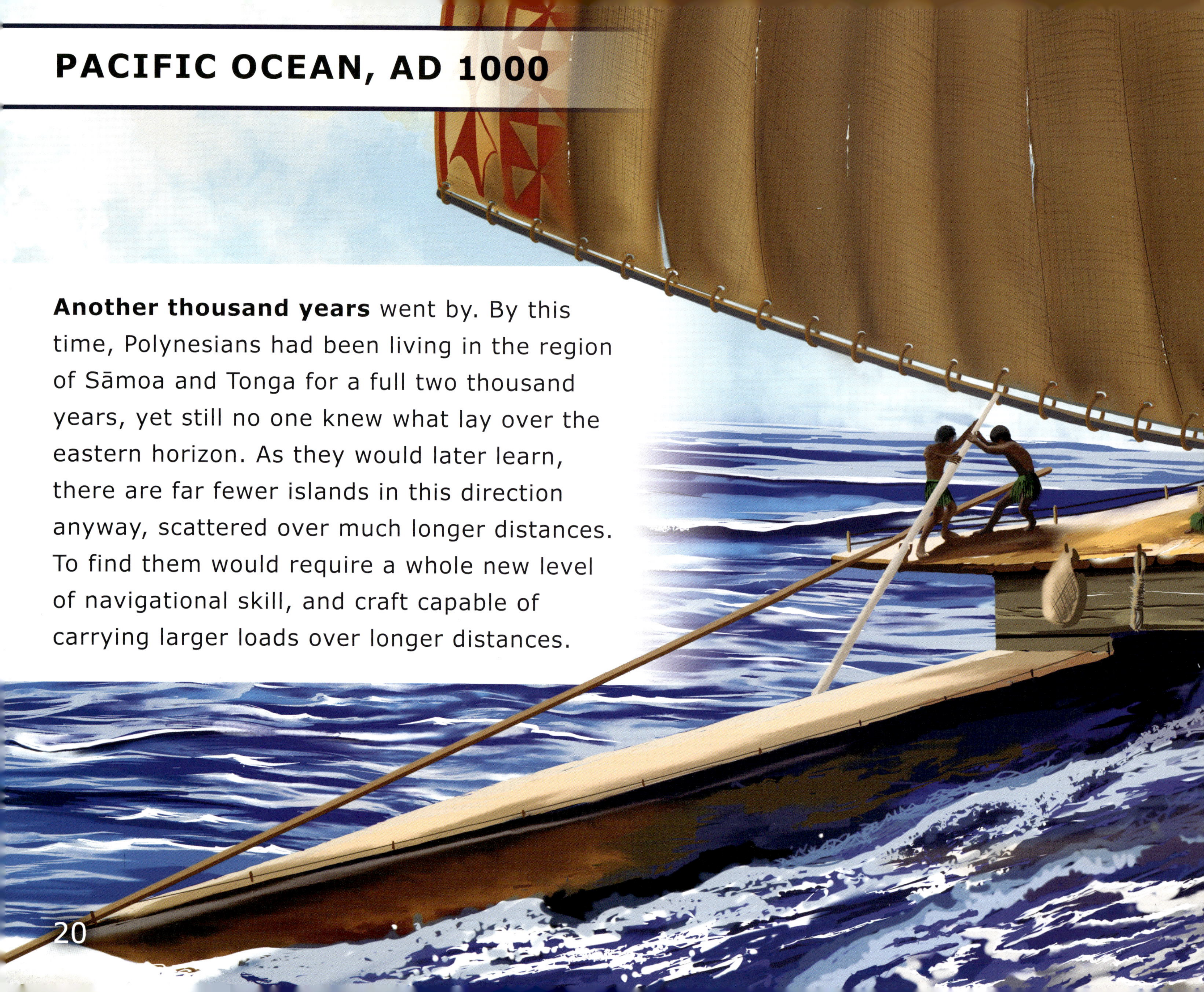

PACIFIC OCEAN, AD 1000

Another thousand years went by. By this time, Polynesians had been living in the region of Sāmoa and Tonga for a full two thousand years, yet still no one knew what lay over the eastern horizon. As they would later learn, there are far fewer islands in this direction anyway, scattered over much longer distances. To find them would require a whole new level of navigational skill, and craft capable of carrying larger loads over longer distances.

By now, Polynesians had begun making double-hulled sailing canoes with a hut built onto a platform to provide some shelter for the crew and their cargo. Whenever an explorer returned with news of a discovery, whole families, chickens, pigs, dogs and plants could be carried over great stretches of ocean to the new island.

Suddenly, Polynesians began finding and settling distant islands in all directions — Rarotonga, Society Islands, Marquesas, Tuamotus, Mangareva and the Hawaiian Islands. To find all of these islands so quickly required a huge level of skill, for the Pacific is vast, the distances very long, and many of the islands are tiny.

Sailing distances

Sāmoa to Rarotonga: 1200 km

Marquesas to Hawai'i: 3500 km

Huge area
These newly discovered islands of 'East Polynesia' are scattered over a huge area almost as big as Africa.

In one of the great achievements of world history, Polynesians expanded their ocean territory by an area almost as large as Africa, and all this in just 250 years or so.

More landfinding birds

For much of the year, sooty terns are out roaming the ocean, but when the season comes for them to nest, they will return to land, providing voyagers with a useful wayfinding clue.

MEANWHILE, OVER ON THE OTHER SIDE OF THE WORLD

Meanwhile, over on the other side of the world, Viking sailors from Norway had also begun sailing well out of sight of land. Heading for the Faroe Islands, north of Scotland, they missed and came to Iceland — a much larger, mountainous island. From here, they would go on to find the world's largest island of Greenland, before taking another hop to reach the islands of northern Canada.

Greenland
Canada
Norway
Iceland
Viking voyaging

Sailing distances

Norway to Faroe: 580 km

Faroe to Iceland: 440 km

Iceland to Greenland: 300 km

Greenland to Canada: 30+ km

CANADA

Compared with most islands in the Pacific, all these targets — Iceland, Greenland and Canada — were huge and the distances to reach them were relatively short.

GREENLAND
ICELAND
FAROE ISLANDS
NORWAY
SCOTLAND

Kamal — a simple navigational device used by the Arabs around this time to gauge the positions of the stars.

By this time, navigators on both sides of the Arabian Sea were regularly steering a shortcut between ports in Africa and India.

The Chinese were sailing further from the coast, too, with the help of a simple kind of compass.

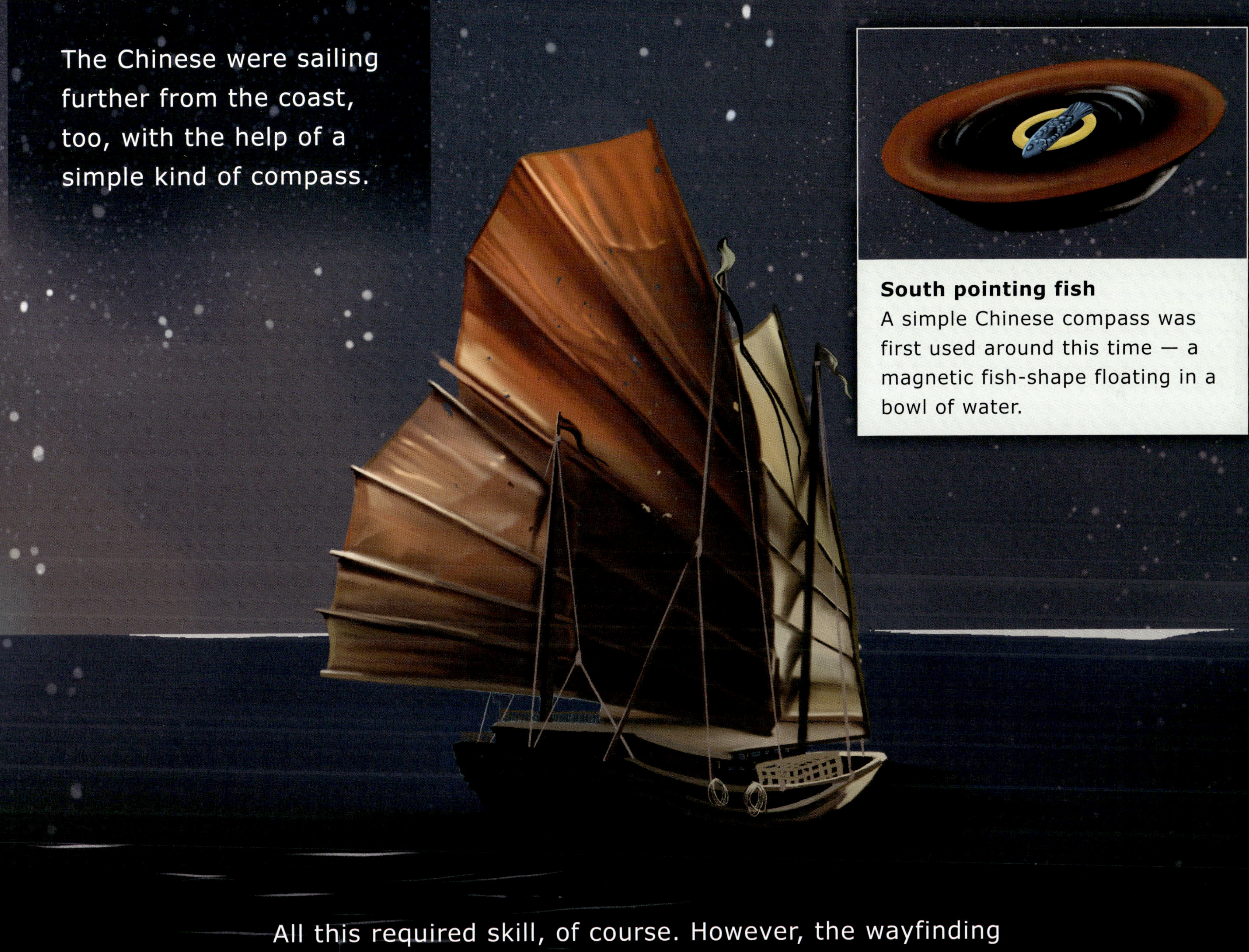

South pointing fish
A simple Chinese compass was first used around this time — a magnetic fish-shape floating in a bowl of water.

All this required skill, of course. However, the wayfinding abilities of Pacific sailors were still far more advanced.

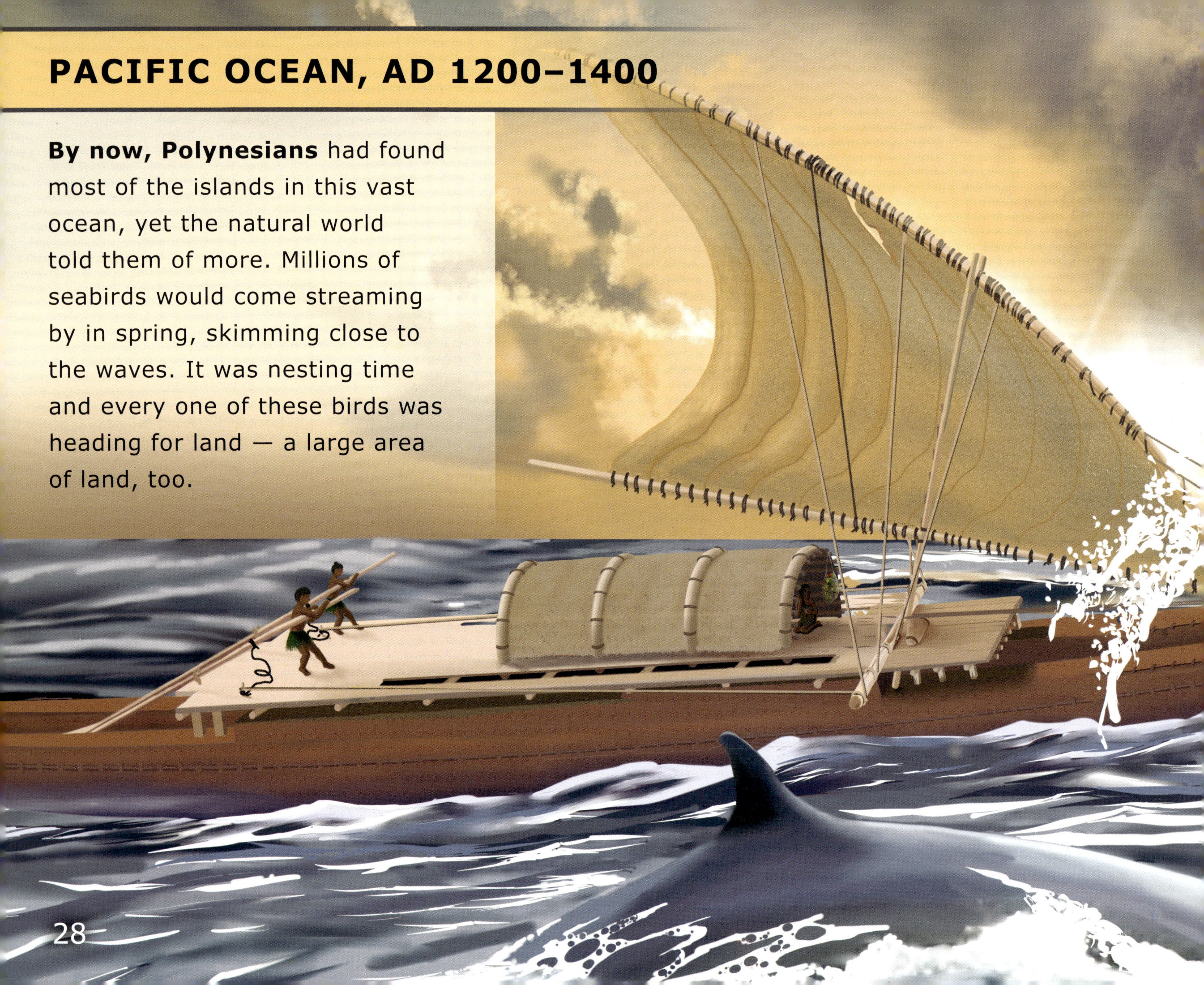

PACIFIC OCEAN, AD 1200–1400

By now, Polynesians had found most of the islands in this vast ocean, yet the natural world told them of more. Millions of seabirds would come streaming by in spring, skimming close to the waves. It was nesting time and every one of these birds was heading for land — a large area of land, too.

The sailors compared this direction with where the sun went down, the positions of rising and setting stars, and the direction of the winds and ocean swell. They kept an eye out, too, for passing birds and whales.

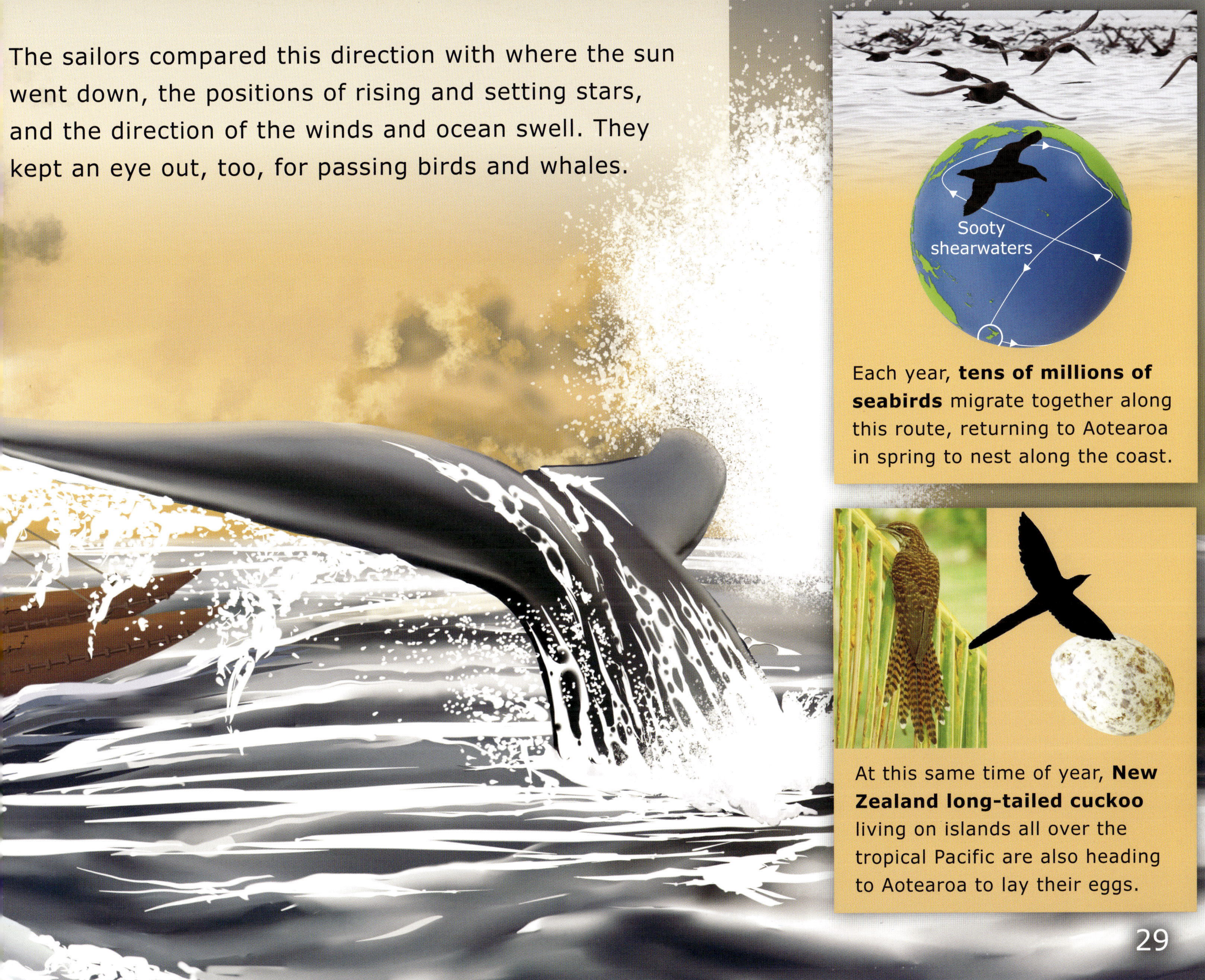

Each year, **tens of millions of seabirds** migrate together along this route, returning to Aotearoa in spring to nest along the coast.

At this same time of year, **New Zealand long-tailed cuckoo** living on islands all over the tropical Pacific are also heading to Aotearoa to lay their eggs.

PACIFIC OCEAN, AD 1250

After weeks at sea, the voyagers saw driftwood, seaweed and a long white cloud. Sailing on, they came to the last big area of habitable land on Earth: Aotearoa.

The first people to reach this new land arrived around AD 1250. Most, if not all, had left from the region of the Society Islands or Cook Islands.

On reaching Aotearoa, some sailed right around the North Island, while others took shortcuts across it, dragging their canoes overland from one coast to the other. Still others headed further south to explore the South Island, Stewart Island, the Chatham Islands and Enderby Island.

Canoe shortcuts

Shown in red are two of the many coast-to-coast canoe shortcuts (portage routes) used by Māori: Waitematā to Manukau and Tāmaki River to Manukau.

Around this same time, Polynesians set off on an even greater adventure to find and settle one of the most remote islands in the world: Rapa Nui (Easter Island).

How did they move these statues? It seems that Polynesians 'walked' them along with ropes, in much the same way that they 'walked' heavy canoes up the beach.

Sailing distances
Ecuador to Marquesas:
6500 km

Kūmara voyages
The original Pacific kūmara and its name come from Ecuador, South America.

From here, they continued to the South American coastline to reach Ecuador, where they tasted their first kūmara. Collecting some tubers — and a few new crew members — they sailed back into the Pacific for at least a month before they saw land again.

Remarkably, Polynesians would go on to distribute this crop over truly enormous distances to establish it on Rapa Nui, the Hawaiian Islands and Aotearoa.

MEANWHILE, OVER ON THE OTHER SIDE OF THE WORLD

Meanwhile, over on the other side of the world, Mediterranean sailors had learnt to reach familiar ports and harbours on the far side of their sea more reliably with the help of a dry mariner's compass and special maps known as portolan charts.

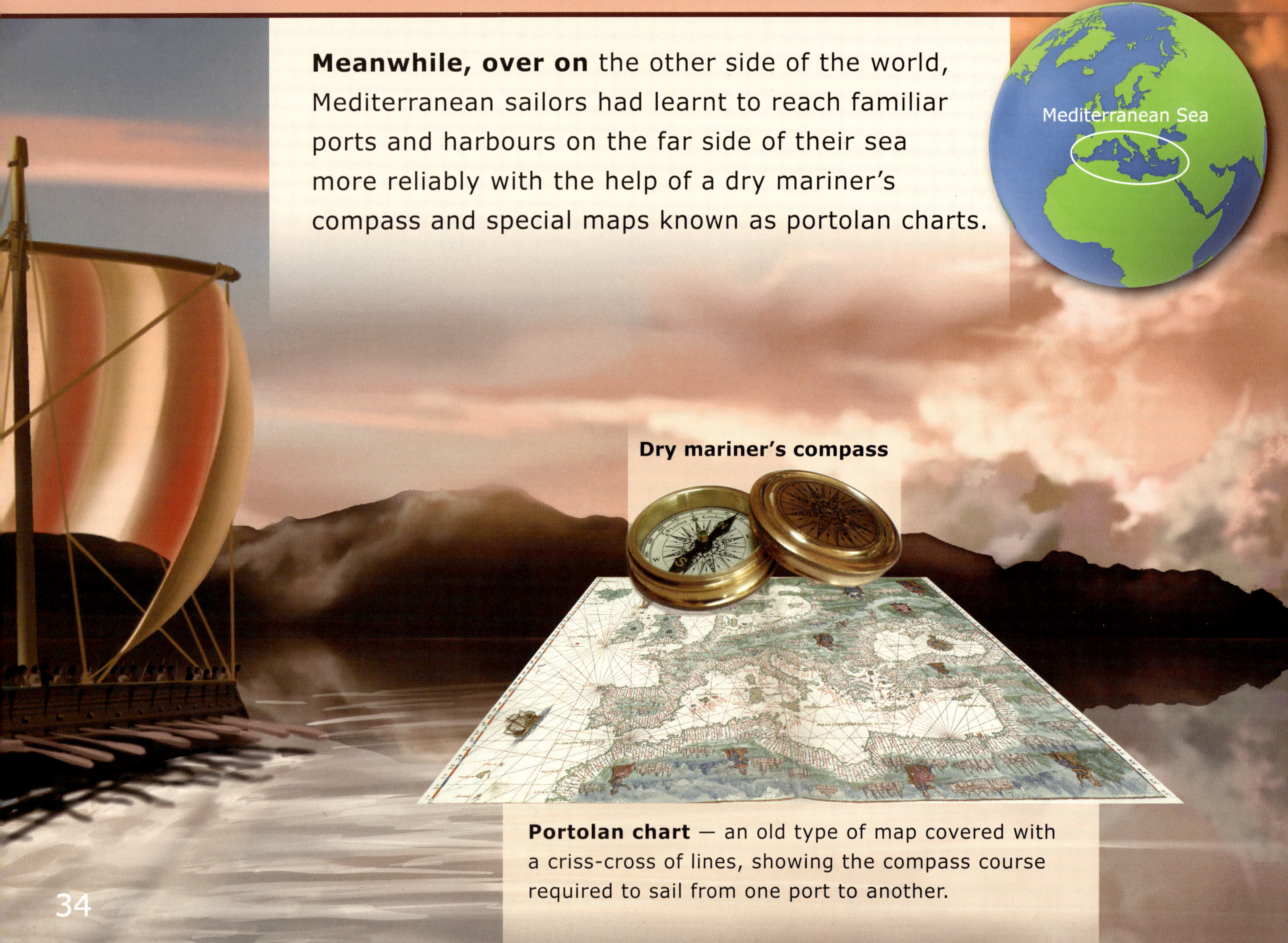

Dry mariner's compass

Portolan chart — an old type of map covered with a criss-cross of lines, showing the compass course required to sail from one port to another.

The Chinese were building huge, four-masted ships and sailing them along known shipping routes for even longer distances, as far as Africa. Unlike the Polynesians, though, neither were searching for small targets or finding new land.

PACIFIC OCEAN, AD 1500

By this time, Polynesians had settled most of the Pacific, yet they still continued to voyage back and forth between the islands to trade in stone and shells for making tools, to carry decorative feathers and to distribute crop plants.

Canoe cargo
Items carried aboard the canoes (often for thousands of kilometres) include red-feathered birds and their feathers (for cloaks and headdresses), kūmara, bottle gourds and seeds, candlenuts (for lighting), and karaka seeds (for planting).

More items of cargo
A flake of obsidian for cutting, a stone adze blade, an auger shell to make a chisel, and a pearlshell for making fishhooks and lures.

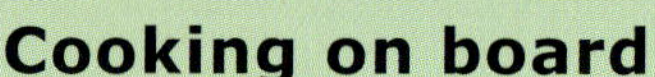

Cooking on board
Sometimes, a fire would be lit on board on a bed of sand.

Then, suddenly, most of this long-distance voyaging stopped. Polynesians were no longer finding new land. With the onset of fighting over territory and resources, newcomers were not always welcome, making voyaging more dangerous.

MEANWHILE, OVER ON THE OTHER SIDE OF THE WORLD

Meanwhile, over on the other side of the world, European sailors were getting ready to make a really long, open-sea voyage of their own. Rather than follow the long hard road to Asia overland, they decided to try reaching Asia from the other side by sailing west.

Old overland route to Asia (1270 Marco Polo)

Marco Polo's journey
Marco Polo's overland journey to Asia took him almost four years — and that's just one way!

GULF OF MEXICO

THE BAHAMAS

CUBA

PUERTO RICO

CARIBBEAN SEA

In 1492, Christopher Columbus left Spain with three ships, a maritime compass and a quadrant. To check how far he had sailed, he would throw something light over the side to see how fast it drifted by, measuring the passing hours with a sandglass.

After five weeks at sea, he reached land. It was not Asia, though, but America. Indeed, this is how the first islands off America came to be known as the West Indies and the native people of the region became known as American Indians.

Navigational tools
A quadrant for measuring the height of the sun and stars, a compass for measuring direction, and a sandglass for measuring time.

The ships of European explorers couldn't simply be dragged overland like a Polynesian canoe, so they had to find a way around America instead.

In 1519, Portuguese navigator Ferdinand Magellan headed south for a month until he found a deep inlet. He followed this inland, tasting the water as he went. Finding it salty, he knew that he had found a route through to a 'new sea', a sea that he would name Mar Pacifico (the 'peaceful sea' or Pacific Ocean).

PACIFIC OCEAN, 1521

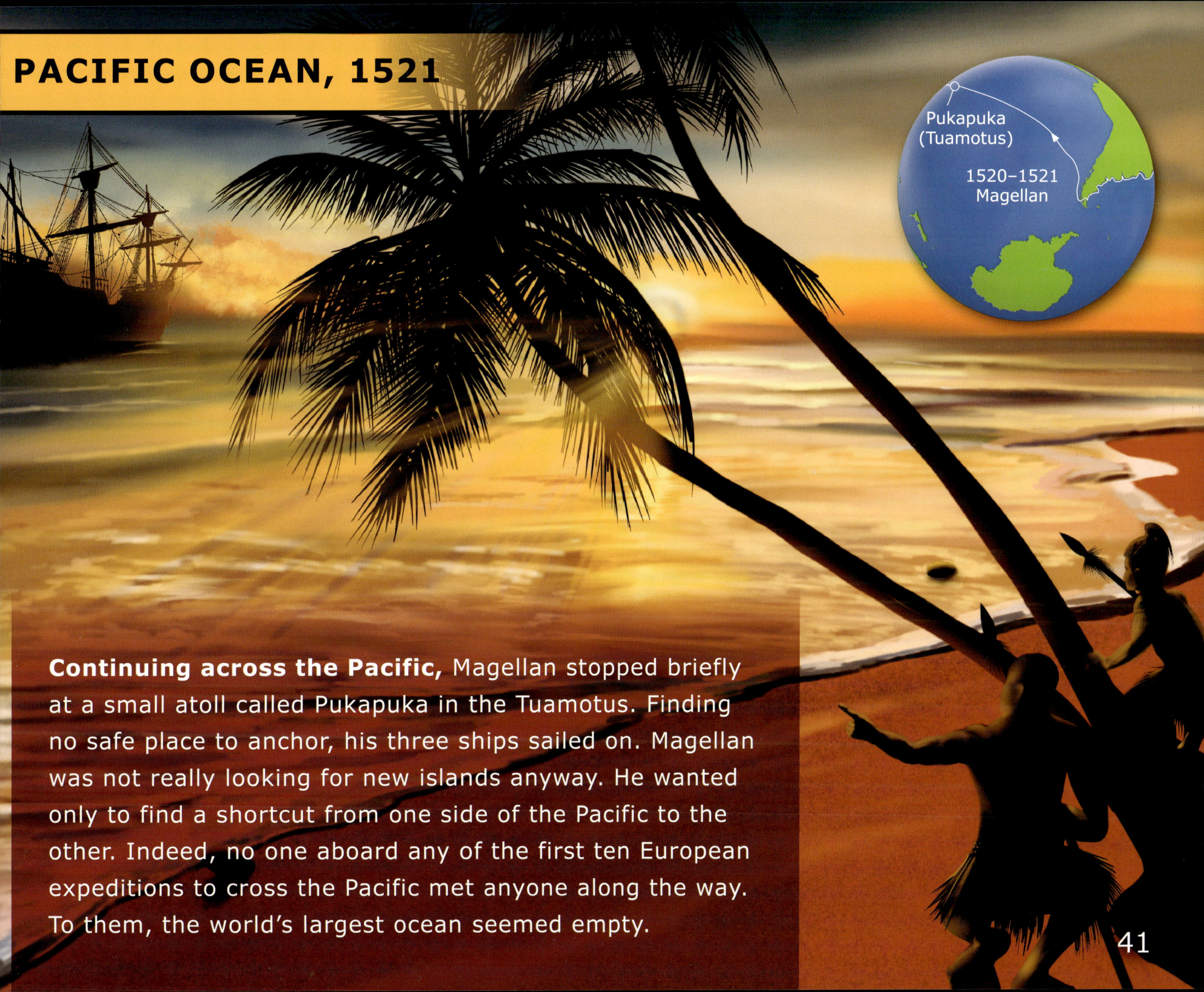

Continuing across the Pacific, Magellan stopped briefly at a small atoll called Pukapuka in the Tuamotus. Finding no safe place to anchor, his three ships sailed on. Magellan was not really looking for new islands anyway. He wanted only to find a shortcut from one side of the Pacific to the other. Indeed, no one aboard any of the first ten European expeditions to cross the Pacific met anyone along the way. To them, the world's largest ocean seemed empty.

PACIFIC OCEAN, 1595

All this would change on 21 July 1595. That day, the people of Fatu Hiva in the Marquesas Islands saw four strange ships appear. Some 400 islanders crowded into outrigger canoes and paddled out to meet them. There were 378 men, women and children aboard, all desperate for provisions after more than three months at sea. The islanders brought them fresh food and drinking water before welcoming the crew ashore.

In exchange, the Marquesans began taking things. The Spanish commander objected, ordering that a warning shot be fired. Stunned by the sound, the islanders began leaping overboard, for they had never seen nor heard a gun before.

These strange blasts continued to ring out across the bay. By the time the newcomers had left, more than 200 islanders had been killed.

It was the first known meeting between a Polynesian and a European, a tragic one that would be remembered forever.

PACIFIC OCEAN, 1606

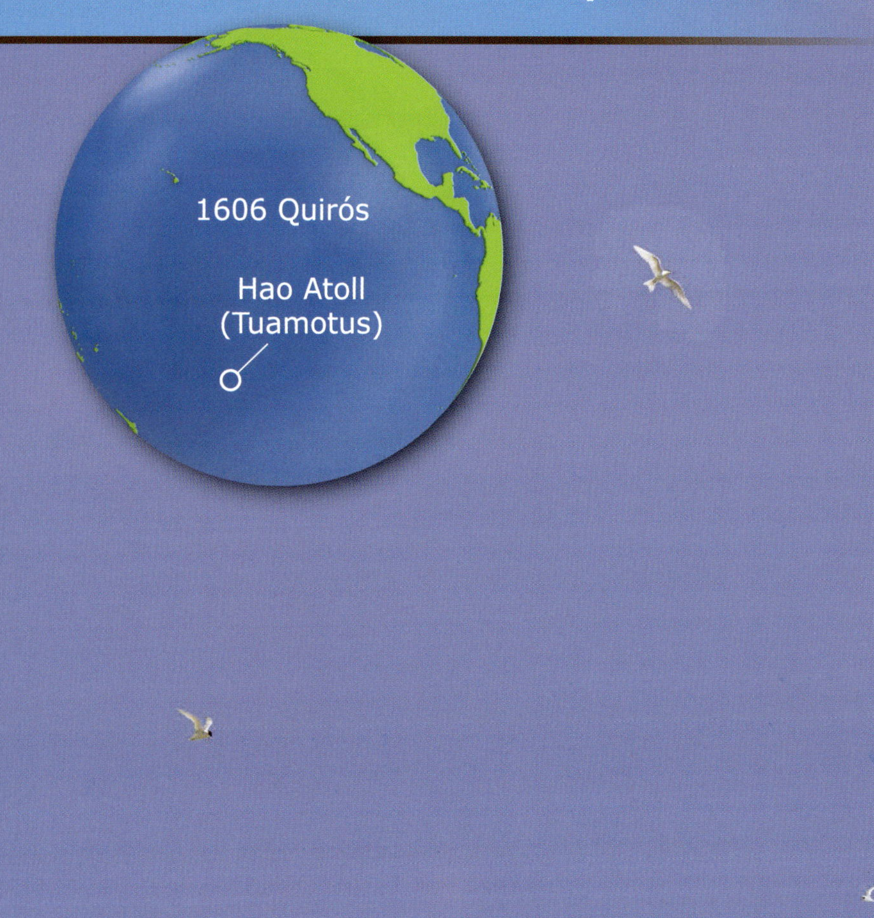

Eleven years passed before the people of Hao in the Tuamotus saw two more ships approach. They quickly lit a fire as a warning and lined up along the beach with clubs and lances, cautiously signalling to the Spanish crew to land.

As a sign of friendship, the chief presented a palm branch, beckoning the 160 pale-skinned men into the village to eat. After almost two months at sea, the visitors were particularly glad of the fresh coconut water they were offered.

Indeed, the islanders were always quick to understand the need of newcomers, yet also had to protect their own people and food supply. This is why they would often offer a ritual challenge.

This time things went well, but Europeans would often make the tragic mistake of taking these challenges as a call to fight.

PACIFIC OCEAN, 1616

Ten years on and Polynesians were far out at sea when they saw another strange ship on the horizon, this time a Dutch one.

PACIFIC OCEAN — AOTEAROA, 1642

Then, in 1642, another Dutchman entered the Pacific. His two ships anchored off the north-west coast of New Zealand's South Island, where local Māori challenged them with a haka and shell trumpet call. Unsure how to respond, Abel Tasman's men answered with their own trumpet, getting their guns and swords ready. A conflict broke out and the Dutch fled north to Tonga and Fiji. Again, neither side had understood the other.

PACIFIC OCEAN — RAPA NUI, 1722

Eighty years passed, then another Dutchman entered the Pacific. Jacob Roggeveen had his hopes set on finding a Great Southern Continent, but found Rapa Nui (Easter Island) instead. Here, he was greatly impressed by the health of the islanders and by their enormous stone statues. He noted the abundance of their crops and their generous offer to supply a whole heap of sugarcane, about sixty chickens, yams and thirty bunches of bananas. And yet here again there were misunderstandings. Roggeveen's men fired some 35 shots at the islanders, needlessly killing ten or more.

Terra Australis, the great southern continent that never existed
The search for a 'Great Southern Continent' was based on a belief that land on the northern side of the planet should be balanced by land in the south. It even appeared on early maps.

PACIFIC OCEAN — TAHITI, 1767

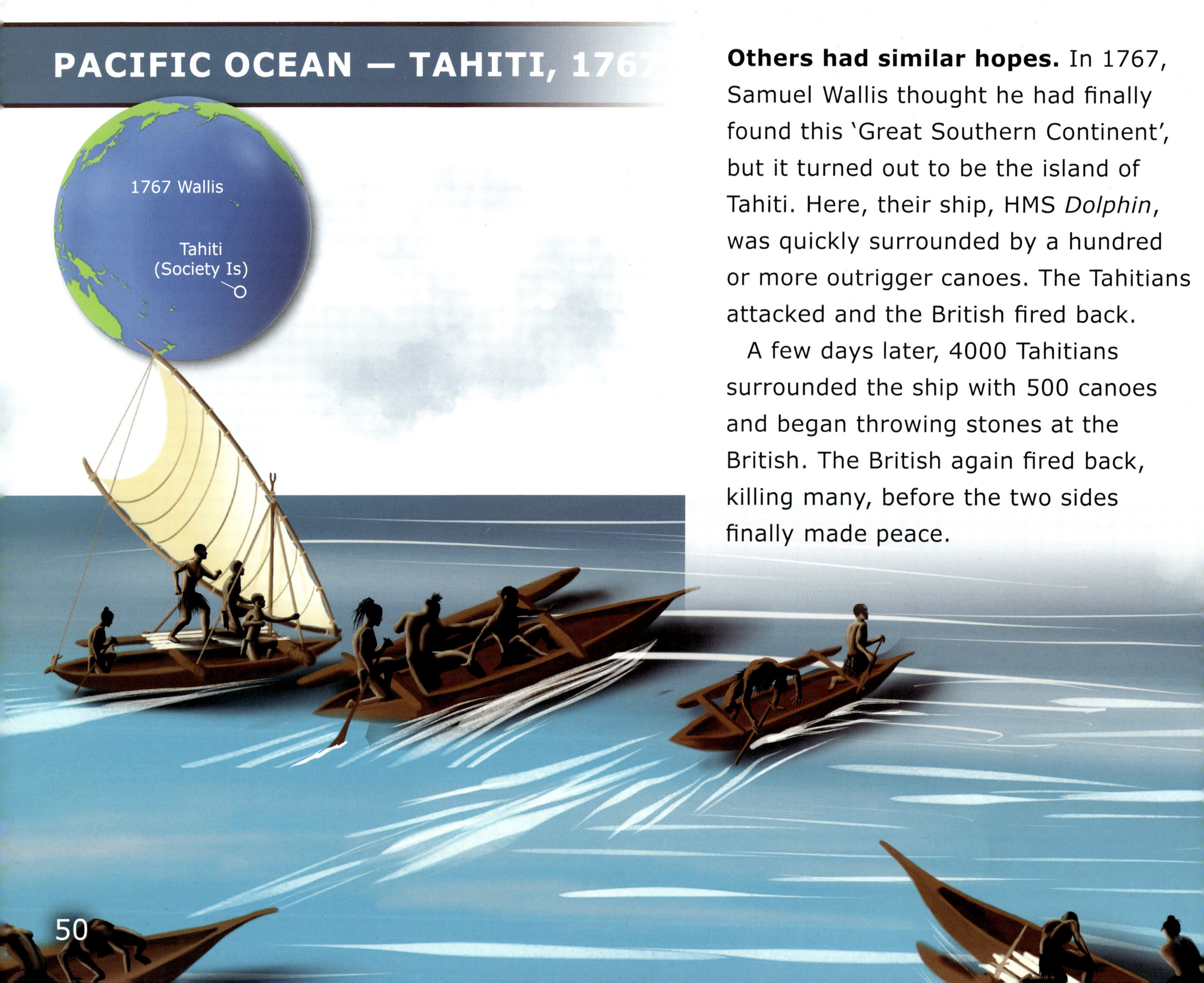

Others had similar hopes. In 1767, Samuel Wallis thought he had finally found this 'Great Southern Continent', but it turned out to be the island of Tahiti. Here, their ship, HMS *Dolphin*, was quickly surrounded by a hundred or more outrigger canoes. The Tahitians attacked and the British fired back.

A few days later, 4000 Tahitians surrounded the ship with 500 canoes and began throwing stones at the British. The British again fired back, killing many, before the two sides finally made peace.

PACIFIC OCEAN — TAHITI, 1768

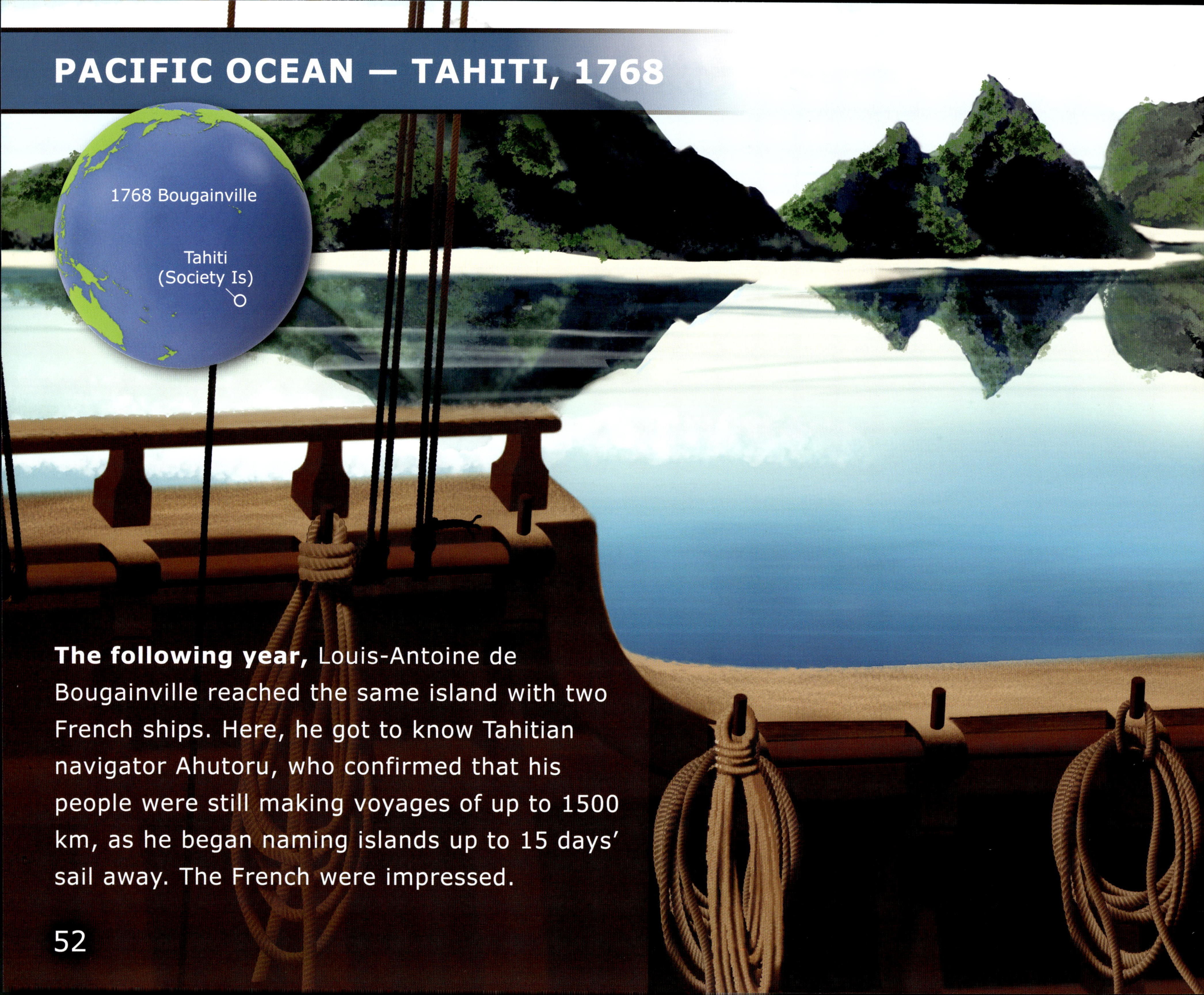

The following year, Louis-Antoine de Bougainville reached the same island with two French ships. Here, he got to know Tahitian navigator Ahutoru, who confirmed that his people were still making voyages of up to 1500 km, as he began naming islands up to 15 days' sail away. The French were impressed.

It seems that Ahutoru was also impressed, for he asked to join Bougainville's voyage. Here, he continued to inspire the crew with his navigational skill and knowledge of astronomy.

PACIFIC OCEAN — TAHITI, 1769

British Captain James Cook followed. On reaching Tahiti, he met Tupaia, another master navigator, who described to him nearly 130 islands, giving the sailing directions to 74 of them. From this information, Cook even tried to make his own map.

Just as Ahutoru had sailed on to Paris with Bougainville, Tupaia agreed to join Cook. Tupaia soon astonished everyone on board. No matter how far they sailed together — to Aotearoa and Australia — he could always point accurately back to his home island. It was a skill that no one could explain.

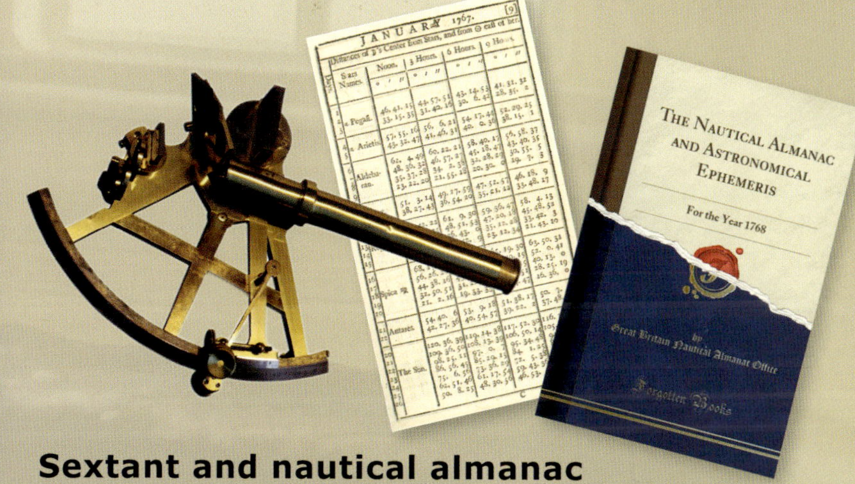

Sextant and nautical almanac
For Cook to work out where he was, he had to use charts that gave the angular distance between any major star and the moon, and the height of that star and moon above the horizon. He would then compare these figures with observations he made with his sextant. (At this stage, on his first voyage, he still didn't have a clock that could keep accurate time at sea.)

PACIFIC OCEAN — HAWAI‘I, 1778
The islands
of Hawai‘i
Polynesia

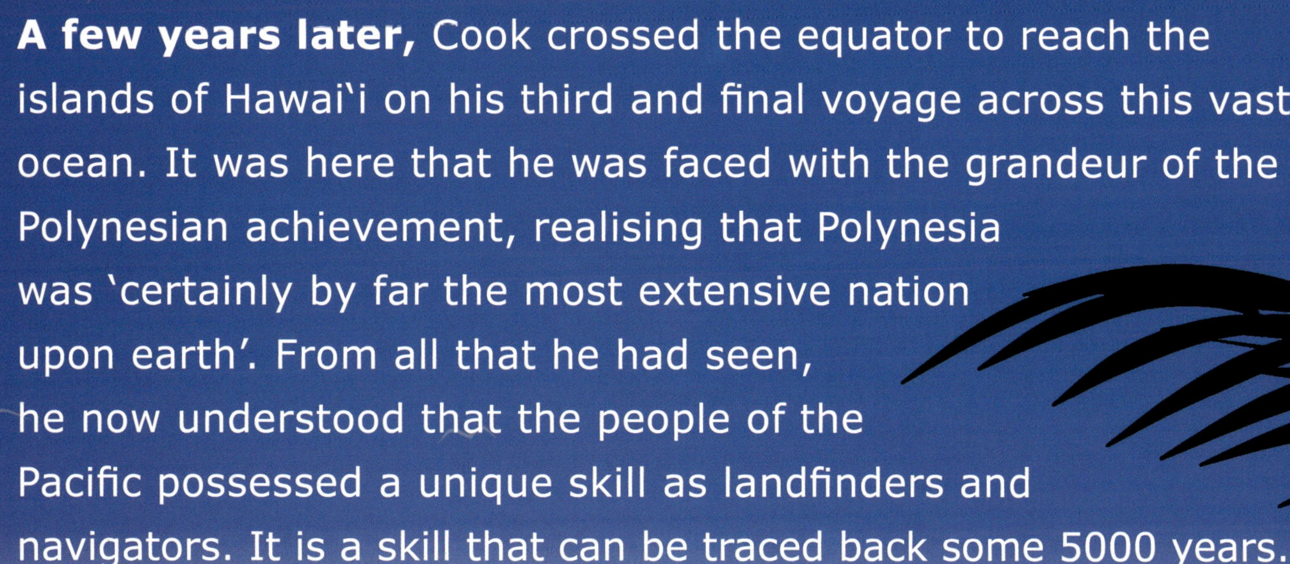

A few years later, Cook crossed the equator to reach the islands of Hawai'i on his third and final voyage across this vast ocean. It was here that he was faced with the grandeur of the Polynesian achievement, realising that Polynesia was 'certainly by far the most extensive nation upon earth'. From all that he had seen, he now understood that the people of the Pacific possessed a unique skill as landfinders and navigators. It is a skill that can be traced back some 5000 years.

latitude or twelve hundred leagues
And eighty-three degrees of long
hundred and sixty leagues east
How much farther in either direction its colonies reach is not known; but what we know already, in consequence of this and our former voyage, warrants our pronouncing it to be, though perhaps not the most numerous, certainly, by far, the most extensive nation upon earth.

Cook understood

In Captain Cook's journal, he clearly records his sense of awe at the grandeur of the Polynesian achievement.

The story does not end here, though!

TODAY

These days, voyaging societies are springing up on islands right across the Pacific. We can be grateful to them, for they help to share and celebrate these remarkable old wayfinding skills.

Pacific voyaging societies
So far, Pacific voyaging societies have been set up in Fiji, Aotearoa, Hawaiʻi, Tahiti, Tonga, Sāmoa and Cook Islands.

Hōkūleʻa
The *Hōkūleʻa* of the Polynesian Voyaging Society of Hawaiʻi, which recently circumnavigated the globe. The voyage took three years and covered 87,000 kilometres with stops at 85 ports in 26 countries.

To this day, the original multi-hull boatbuilding styles of the Pacific people continue to inspire others. Indeed, the record for the world's fastest ever deep-ocean sailing craft is currently held by a multi-hull.

***IDEC SPORT*, the world's fastest ocean-going sailing craft**
In 2017, this 31.5-metre trimaran set a record for the fastest circumnavigation of the world by any type of yacht by sailing right around the world in just 40 days, 23 hours, 30 minutes and 30 seconds, averaging 26.9 knots (49.8 kph).

EXPLORATION TIMELINE

Polynesia's Age of Exploration

3000 BC	Ancestors of Polynesians explore the South China Sea
1500 BC	Ancestors of Polynesians reach the Bismarck Islands
900 BC	First people arrive in the region of Tonga and Sāmoa
AD 1000	Polynesians settle much of East Polynesia
AD 1250	Polynesians have settled Rapa Nui and Aotearoa
AD 1450	Polynesians stop much of their long-distance voyaging

A scene from the Society Islands, 1769.

Followed by . . .

Europe's Age of Exploration (Finding new trade routes and places already inhabited by others)

1492	Christopher Columbus of Italy crosses the Atlantic to America
1498	Vasco da Gama of Portugal finds his way around Africa to reach India
1521	Ferdinand Magellan of Portugal crosses the Pacific
1595	Alvaro de Mendaña of Spain finds the people of the Marquesas Islands
1606	Pedro Fernandes de Quirós of Portugal finds the people of the Tuamotus and Rakahanga (Northern Cook Is)
1616	Willem Schouten and Isaac Le Maire of Holland find the people of Tonga and Futuna (and visit the Tuamotus)
1642	Abel Janszoon Tasman of Holland finds the Māori people of Aotearoa (also visits Tonga and sights Fiji)
1722	Jacob Roggeveen of Holland finds the people of Rapa Nui and Sāmoa (and visits the Tuamotus)
1765	John Byron of England finds the people of Pukapuka (Northern Cook Is) (and visits the Tuamotus)
1767	Samuel Wallis of England finds the people of both Tahiti and 'Uvea (Wallis Is) (and visits the Tuamotus)
1768	Louis-Antoine de Bougainville of France visits the Tuamotus, Tahiti and Sāmoa
1769	James Cook of England visits Tahiti and Aotearoa; Jean-François de Surville of France visits Aotearoa
1778	James Cook of England finds the people of the Hawaiian Islands

CHANCE OR SKILL?

A few still question whether the Polynesian achievement required any special landfinding or navigational skill, believing that their settlements were the result of fishing trips gone wrong or desperate people in fully-laden voyaging canoes fleeing into the unknown. For them, here are a few things to consider:

1) The Pacific covers one third of the planet and yet almost every habitable island in it was discovered, settled and planted out with food crops well before Europeans arrived. And the last phase of this expansion — an area the size of Africa — was fast.
2) Several master navigators from atolls in the Western Pacific have maintained their original non-instrument navigational skills and can still demonstrate them. Indeed, these skills continue to be taught and practiced by voyaging societies today.
3) Cook's Tahitian navigator, Tupaia, gave several convincing demonstrations to the crew of the *Endeavour* of his uncanny navigational skill, including the ability to provide star courses to 74 islands. Archaeological evidence also confirms sophisticated sailing technology.
4) Evidence of return voyaging, including the impressive long-distance distribution of the Ecuadorian kūmara to Rapa Nui, Aotearoa and the Hawaiian Islands.

BACKGROUND NOTES AND SOURCES

Pages 2–3: The origins of Polynesians can be traced back to a region bounded by Taiwan, the Philippines and Indonesia. The South China Sea is 3,500,000 km^2 and the Mediterranean Sea is 2,500,000 km^2.

Pages 6–7: Lapita pottery is named after the place in New Caledonia where fragments were first identified.

Page 9: The oldest-known remains of plank boats found in the region of the English Channel date to 1500 BC, e.g., the so-called Dover Bronze Age Boat. Unfortunately, no evidence has yet been found to indicate how these boats were propelled.

Pages 10–11: The first settlers of this region had reached Tonga by 900 BC. In this region, Pacific pigeons (Lupe) regularly migrate between the islands, and their landfinding role is commemorated in the creation myths of Sāmoa.

Pages 22–23: According to the most recent dating evidence, the first people to reach East Polynesia had arrived by around AD 1000.

Pages 24–25: (The first people to settle the Faroe Islands evidently arrived at least 300 years earlier, possibly from the Shetland Islands, 290 km away.) Although Polynesians are sometimes considered the Vikings of the Pacific, this fails to give due recognition to the Pacific people for their undeniably superior landfinding skills.

Pages 26–27: There is evidence from around this time of coastal trading links between China and the Mediterranean. During this period, the ancestors of Malagasy evidently made their way from Indonesia to the island of Madagascar along a similar route.

Pages 28–29: In spring, as many as 20 million sooty shearwaters head from rich fishing grounds in the North Pacific across the equator to pass like a river through East Polynesia, making use of a seasonal change in the winds as they skim the waves, on migration towards Aotearoa. The navigational observation of such phenomenon is referred to in at least one traditional Polynesian voyaging chant.

Page 30: The first people to settle in Aotearoa arrived around AD 1250. Most are understood to have arrived from, or via, the Society, Austral and Cook Islands.

Page 31: The use of a portage (canoe shortcut) from Waitematā Harbour to the Manukau Harbour is recorded for *Tainui* waka.

Page 32: The latest dating evidence from Rapa Nui (Easter Island) suggests that the first people to settle had arrived by around AD 1200 — most likely from Mangareva.

Page 33: Although Native Americans are known to have used seagoing balsa rafts to sail along the Andean Coast, it is generally agreed that they are unlikely to have been responsible for introducing this crop to Polynesia. This is largely due to a lack of convincing motive to risk downwind voyages into the unknown over such immense distances, and a lack of evidence that they possessed the requisite off-shore landfinding and navigational skills, or the island environment in which to develop them. Scholars now generally agree that this crop was introduced by Polynesian gardeners reaching the coast of South America via Rapa Nui. While DNA evidence confirms early Native American presence in the Pacific, the most credible explanation is that these people reached there aboard a Polynesian craft navigated by Polynesians. See *Science* 369.6500 (2020): 128, and *Pathway of the Birds* by Andrew Crowe.

Page 35: From 1405 to 1433, Chinese commander Zheng He led a huge fleet of ships as far west as Africa. Gavin Menzies (in *1421: The Year China Discovered the World*) claimed that Zheng He also crossed the Pacific, a claim dismissed by professional Chinese historians as fanciful and lacking any sound basis.

Pages 36–37: By AD 1450, most long-distance voyaging had stopped. Around the same time, two major tsunami are known to have occurred. Fortifications (pā), like this one shown in Aotearoa, began to be built around AD 1500.

Page 41: Magellan is known to have passed close to inhabited atolls, including nearby Nāpuka. Of the ten expeditions that followed Magellan, one possible exception to a lack of contact lies with the crew of *San Lesmes* of García Jofre de Loaísa's expedition from Spain, a craft that evidently sank in the same region in 1526.

Pages 42–45: From *The Voyages of Pedro Fernandez de Quiros, 1595 to 1606*. [Note however that the editor misidentifies the atoll of Hao as 'Ana'a]

Page 46: From *The Australian Navigations of Jacob le Maire*.

Page 47: From *Abel Janszoon Tasman's Journal*.

Pages 48–49: From Jacob Roggeveen's journal.

Pages 50–51: From *The Discovery of Tahiti, A Journal of the Second Voyage of H.M.S.* Dolphin *Round the World*.

Pages 52–53: From *A Voyage Round the World* by Louis-Antoine de Bougainville.

Pages 54–57: From *The Journals of Captain James Cook* and from *Observations Made During a Voyage Round the World* by Johann Reinhold Forster.

Inside back cover: Although the original people of the Pacific were all voyagers, Polynesia stands out as a distinct region because of shared customs, language, DNA and the overall extent of their voyaging.

USEFUL BOOKS AND WEBSITES

Websites of the various voyaging societies based in Aotearoa, Hawai'i, Tahiti, Tonga, Sāmoa, Cook Islands and Fiji.

The Encyclopedia of New Zealand. 'Pacific migrations' by Geoff Irwin in https://teara.govt.nz/en/pacific-migrations

The Adventures of Tupaia by Courtney Sina Meredith and Mat Tait. Allen & Unwin, Auckland, 2019.

Pathway of the Birds: The voyaging achievements of Māori and their Polynesian ancestors by Andrew Crowe. Bateman Books, Auckland (University of Hawai'i Press, Honolulu), 2018.

Reawakened: Traditional navigators of Te Moana-nui-a-Kiwa by Jeff Evans. Massey University Press, Auckland, 2021.

Tupaia: The remarkable story of Captain Cook's Polynesian navigator by Joan Druett. Random House, Auckland, 2012.

Vaka Moana: Voyages of the Ancestors — The discovery and settlement of the Pacific edited by Kerry Howe. Bateman Books, Auckland, 2006.

Vikings of the Sunrise by Te Rangi Hīroa (Sir Peter Henry Buck). F. A. Stokes Co., New York, 1938, and Whitcombe & Tombs, Christchurch, 1954.

INDEX

ACKNOWLEDGEMENTS

The impetus for this book came from many quarters. In particular, I would like to acknowledge 'Tuia Encounters 250', a national event in Aotearoa tasked with celebrating 'the meeting of two great voyaging traditions', and Professor David Tipene-Leach, who gently insisted that my earlier book *Pathway of the Birds* be adapted for young children. My quest for the right illustrator finally bore fruit through the inspiration of children's librarian, Shori Allan. Thank you and to Rick, and to all those contributing to the various Pacific voyaging trusts, including Te Toki. Kia kaha! Through you, the world is reminded of some of the greatest achievements of Pacific people!

Andrew Crowe, Aotearoa 2023

Kia mau mana ai tātau

(May we all carry ourselves with dignity)

PHOTO CREDITS

Page 7, Metropolitan Museum of Art (pottery); page 11, Peter van der Sluijs (fish), Evan-Amos (banana), Rajeshodayanchal (breadfruit), Yongxinge (taro), HRajib (coconut); page 16, Diego Delso (frigatebird flying), John Picken (perched); page 23, Duncan Wright (sooty tern), Lieutenant Elizabeth Crapo (colony); page 29, Marlin Harms (shearwaters), G. McCormack/ CINHT (cuckoo), B. Gill (egg); page 32, Terry L. Hunt (photo); page 33, Graham Harris (kūmara); page 34, Richard Nevell (compass), anonymous Portuguese cartographer (map); page 36, Andrew Crowe (lorikeet), Prosperosity (kūmara), David E Mead (candlenuts), Sergio Andres Segovia (gourd), Roger Culos (gourd seeds), Andrew Crowe (berries), Auckland War Memorial Museum (obsidian, adze, lure), H. Zell (*Terebra* shell), Eio-cos (fishhook), James St. John (pearl shell); page 49, Abraham Ortelius (map); page 55, Rama (sextant); page 57, Jacques Reich (portrait of Cook); page 58, Polynesian Voyaging Society (*Hōkūle'a*); page 59, Claude PERON (*IDEC Sport*); page 64, Forest & Kim Starr (white tern).

Published in 2023 by David Bateman Ltd,
Unit 2/5 Workspace Drive, Hobsonville,
Auckland 0618, New Zealand
www.batemanbooks.co.nz
ISBN: 978-1-77689-038-5

A catalogue record for this book is available from the National Library of New Zealand.

Design concept, research, picture research, globes, colour maps, bird silhouettes: Andrew Crowe
Book design: Cheryl Smith

Printed in Malaysia